Gioachino
ROSSINI
IL SIGNOR BRUSCHINO
SINFONIA

Edited by
Clark McAlister

Study Score
Partitur

SERENISSIMA MUSIC, INC.

PREFACE

To be as popular as they are, the overtures to Rossini's operas have been treated very poorly by publishers, both Italian and foreign, throughout most of their histories. Even the most recent editions, as thorough as many of them are, do not answer all of the questions concerning textual matters.

It will probably always be so. First, many of the textual inconsistencies one finds come from Rossini's own manuscripts. During most of his career, Rossini was working at an incredibly fast and furious pace, so it is not surprising that some relatively small details would escape his attention. Also, working at such speed inevitably took a toll on the legibility of some of his manuscripts, thereby adding another layer of potential uncertainty. While the context will frequently clarify such matters, in numerous cases different readings are possible.

Second, these scores come from a time when performance practices still assumed that the written score would be modified in performance in certain fairly predictable ways. Broadly speaking, for example, a certain lightness of execution was expected, the notation of which in our own era requires a rather liberal use of staccato dots. In Rossini's time, this refinement of notation was not practiced.

Third, in the case of works written for the stage which were already frequently performed during the composer's lifetime, it is quite logical to believe that Rossini's manuscript scores represent only an intermediate stage in the perfection of his music. The world of opera, more than that of concert music, thrives on revisions and alterations. Many of these changes, of course, are made to suit specific circumstances, and the composer would not want them to become permanent. Norman Del Mar, in his invaluable book *Orchestra Variations*, points out that, on the other hand, some of these changes represent composer-sanctioned second thoughts and even, sometimes, improvements over the original version of the text to be found in the manuscript score. As Del Mar says, "Not all traditions are bad and many derive from the composer himself or the society to which he belonged."

The question, then, becomes how to distinguish one kind of change from the other—when a later source differs from an earlier one, which reading should be followed? If we accept that in many instances no definitive answer is possible, we must follow our best understanding of Rossini's style, both as an individual composer and as one working contentedly within the prevailing performance practices of his time. The present editions of these overtures seek to do just that—by examining as many sources as possible, to arrive at performing texts which both reflect the spirit of the composer and are as practical as possible for the use of modern orchestras.

There is one aspect of this and other scores of Rossini's that needs more clarification than will fit practically in the space of a footnote. One of Rossini's favorite string colors is the rhythmic tapping, or clicking, of the bow against the string, indicated by the instruction **battute**, or "beaten." Some writers (including Christine Amner in *The A to Z of Foreign Musical Terms* and Walter Kolneder in *Auffürungspraxis bei Vivaldi*) feel that this instruction at least implies execution by using the wood of the bow, col legno. But Norman Del Mar, in *A Companion to the Orchestra*, suggests otherwise. In his discussion of the term col legno he writes:

> It is true that if executed honestly with only the wood of the bow very little actual note is heard, and when composers write important note formations col legno, such Berlioz in the Witches' Sabbath movement of *Symphonie fantastique*, the players will generally cheat by turning the bows sideways to that a little of the hair also comes into play. If they cheat too much, only the hair being brought into contact with the strings, this creates a quite different device, which is found constantly in Rossini under the term battute. . . . None of these vertical techniques produces any enormous volume, especially in view of the cautious attitude of the musicians . . .

To this discussion, three further considerations may be added. First, it will be seen that this technique also yields a staccato "sound," so that the use of staccato dots in notating its use is unnecessary. Second, there are passages which lend themselves to this style of playing but for which Rossini did not indicate battute. When, in these editions, the editor suggests the use of this technique the term [battute] will appear, but the composer's staccato indications will be retained. Finally, Rossini is sometimes not clear about when players should return from battute to conventional arco, whether staccato or not. Although the context may seem to make these changeover points evident, in these editions battute will always be "cancelled" by the term arco.

I wish to thank Nancy M. Bradburd of the Philadelphia Orchestra and Clinton F. Nieweg, Librarian (retired) of that Orchestra, for their insights and suggestions during the preparation of these editions. I am most fortunate to be able to partake of their vast experience in these matters.

The Editor
Spring 2014

In the Sinfonia (Overture) to *Il signor bruschino*, the Violin 2 part at mm. 30-32 and similar places carries the instruction *col legno*. It appears that Rossini intended that the players would tap their bows on the tin covers of the candle-holders (arganti) which were universally used to light the stages (and orchestra pits) in the theaters of his time. The modern practice usually has the violinists tapping the frogs of their bows on the lips of their music stands.

However, Rossini places the symbol for these "bow taps" very carefully either on the D-space below the staff or the E-line just above it, depending on the prevailing tonality of the music. This leads one to ponder exactly what effect the composer had in mind. Certainly tapping the bow on a foreign object like a candle-holder is not a pitch-specific event. Was Rossini at this point in his career (1813) searching for a way to notate some other effect which would be played on the instrument—*col legno*, perhaps, or *battute*? Performers must decide for themselves how to execute these effects.

ORCHESTRA

Flute

2 Oboes

2 Clarinets in B-flat

Bassoon

2 Horns in F

Strings

Duration: ca. 5-6 minutes
Premiere: January 27, 1813
Venice, Teatro San Moisé
Voices and Orchestra / Composer?

This study score is an unabridged licensed reprint – in reduced format – of the large conductor's score first issued by Kalmus. The large score and a complete set of parts are available for sale from the Kalmus catalog as number A 1945.

Edwin F. Kalmus, LC
P. O. Box 5011
Boca Raton, FL 33431-0811
Phone: 561-241-6340; 800-434-6340
Fax: 561-241-6347
Website: www.efkalmus.com

IL SIGNOR BRUSCHINO
ossia IL FIGLIO PER AZZARDO
SINFONIA

Gioachino Rossini
Performing edition by Clark McAlister

SERENISSIMA MUSIC, INC.

6

* The sources have no indication of any change in dynamics between the *ff* in m. 55 and the *cresc.* in . 71. But for the *cresc.* in m. 71 to work, there has to be a drop-off in the dynamic level somewhere between mm. 55 and 71. The most logical thing to do is to insert a *p* either at or just after the downbeat of m. 67.

42080

* See footnote to m. 67.

20

42080

24

42080

www.ingramcontent.com/pod-product-compliance
Lightning Source LLC
Chambersburg PA
CBHW081155040426
42445CB00015B/1894